LEADING IN DIGITAL TIMES

DR. RICHIE ACHUKWU

Published By:
Ssali Publishing
www.salipublishing.com

Publishing African Narratives by African Authors

ssalirose@gmail.com
Cell +27 71 726 8717
Editor: Rose Ssali

ISBN 978-1-990901-37-9

Printed in South Africa

THIS BOOK IS dedicated to my Mom, Catherine Achukwu, to
my mother-in-law,Mamzo and to Dr. Mamiki Molapo

To my dear sisters, Chinne, Uk and Stella

To my beloved brother, Rev. Patrick Achukwu

And

To Africa's digital denizens, her citizens who now largely live
Online in the new digital real estate,
A place of ingenuity, dreams and infinite possibilities

To Africa's leaders
Current and emerging
In the political, social and economic realms
Who are embracing change
And implementing it
That Africa may Arise!

ACKNOWLEDGMENTS

I ACKNOWLEDGE, with love and appreciation, my precious wife, Tumi Achukwu.

I am thankful for our sons, Kamsi, Lyke, JD, JD snr. Ifeanyi and Chukky and our daughter, Sarajean. I believe your tomorrows will be brighter if we have great leadership today.

Special gratitude goes to the Prayer Storm family for their love and divinely-appointed support.

I acknowledge, with thanks, my editor and publisher, Rose Ssali, for her care an attention during the publishing of this book.

Change is not waiting for your annual appraisal or your year-end planning system...
Dr. Richie Achukwu

INTRODUCTION

TO FULLY understand the digital landscape of Africa, we must first analyze our current position, where we have come from, and the roadmap ahead towards a more inclusive and engaged online community. To do this, I will describe some of the foundational digital assets that enable any of this to be possible. This is the real estate upon which the digital economy is built. I will outline the fundamental tools that open up the continent to this new world.

It is vital that we look at current contributions by leaders in both the private and public sectors and the roles expected from each. This will shed some perspective on where the focus needs to be in order to drive our collective economies towards this inevitable future. It's also important that governments create an enabling environment that allows for the business community to make possible this new world. The public sector is responsible for the regulation of this new economy in a way that best promotes both ingenuity that sparks this growth as well as the consumer protections that become necessary as a result of this growth.

I will also highlight some of the areas in which we are lagging behind and therefore need deliberate and concerted attention, as well as the opportunities available to turn this dream into a reality. Overall I remain optimistic about the prospects of this young continent to make the most of this new industrial revolution.

Every digital citizen should have a plan and a vision. Before you begin on social media design a blueprint of how you want your overall digital footprint to look to a global audience.
Germany Kent

1

THE DIGITAL REAL ESTATE

THE DIGITAL economy is built on certain foundational values that help to accelerate its growth and development. These values are the pillars of the real estate upon which the new digital world was kickstarted. These digital assets include the underwater fiber optic cables that connect the continent to the rest of the world and allows for data to move freely. These cables are a huge investment, but they have unlocked the incredible potential by allowing wider access to the internet which is the first step towards making the switch to the digital way of life. Internet access is the bare minimum and lastly, speed is a critical factor. Comparing the African digital landscape to the more advanced economies reveals the lagging speeds experienced. An example of this is the comparison between the time it takes to download a 5GB file in Congo as compared to say, Singapore. Faster internet opens up the country to more opportunities and inevitably makes business operations more efficient. In today's world where a lot of the work is being done remotely, reliable internet is quickly becoming a standard necessity for any economy that wants to remain competitive.

However, I must say that while in many discussions about development, Africa is always shown to be the underdog, left behind and not really in the game. Well, perhaps the digital landscape is more level than others; perhaps in this one area, there might be more of the creative minds at play than the manipulative one. Above all, perhaps necessity is the mother of invention. I will share with you several stories that show this to be a matter of fact.

THE MPESA STORY

M-Pesa is the first banking app for mobile phones to be produced in the developing world. It was designed by Safaricom Limited Company in Kenya. The product has received global attention due to its uniqueness, innovativeness, rapid adoption, and the impact it has made to a large population, mostly people who are poor (bottom of pyramid). M-Pesa has many uses, including the transfer of money from person to person, buying airtime, paying utility bills and keeping the money in the M-Pesa account for future use. The product connected a population which was hitherto disconnected from accessing financial services. M-Pesa has contributed significantly to financial profits for the company as well as to societal value in the country. As an early mover in mobile banking in Kenya, Safaricom partnered with other businesses thereby broadening its agent network before competitors came into the scene. M-Pesa is a disruptive innovation. It created a new market and value network, disrupting the existing ones and becoming a major competitor against the established market leaders and alliances in the financial services sector in Kenya.

The M-Pesa digital app has given the unbanked populace an answer to lack of qualifying for banking services, reduced the times spent on queues at the bank and created many jobs and business opportunities. M-Pesa has enabled Kenya to become a cashless society. You can pay for almost all goods via M-Pesa. The money transfer system is now available in several countries in Africa including Uganda, Tanzania and Mozambique.

The SweepSouth Story

Co-founded by Aisha Pandor, SweepSouth is on online home cleaning platform that connects users to vetted and rated domestic workers in their area. It offers businesses and home owners the opportunity to have their business or home cleaned at the press of a button. One can book either an on-demand clean or set up a recurring booking to secure cheaper rates and the same SweepStar each booking. SweepSouth is SA's biggest home cleaning platform with over 12,000 SweepStars, cleaning homes and businesses in the Western Cape, Gauteng, KZN and Nelspruit.

UBER: DRIVING CHANGE

What is Uber? An interesting question, indeed. What is Uber— a taxi service? Not quite. Public transport? Another good guess, but actually, Uber is an app that connects drivers with riders. The inspiration for Uber came when Travis Kalanick and Garrett Camp found themselves stuck in Paris on a snowy evening, unable to find a taxi. They asked themselves: "What if you could request a ride simply by tapping your phone?" The company first launched in 2009 and has been growing ever since. Its main headquarters are in the tech haven of San Francisco, but there are also major offices in London, Sao Paulo, Mexico City and Amsterdam. You can request a ride with Uber in more than 600 cities worldwide. The company is poised to introduce air transport into urban transport using an App UberElevate. Using VTOL (vertical take-off and landing) aircraft, it could cut down on commuting time and provide quick and reliable links between the suburbs and the city – that could mean a two-hour drive through San Francisco is cut to a 15-minute trip, or a 90-minute commute in India turned into a

6-minute one. Using technology, Uber has changed the way we ride, forever.

INDUSTRY LEADERS LEADING CHANGE

Google has embarked on a project to spread wireless internet across Africa using 4G enabled balloons that float around and give off Wi-Fi signals to communities that might ordinarily have been locked out. Internet access is really a basic need and it's important for every government to make the necessary investment to ensure that everyone, particularly students, are getting good enough exposure to empower themselves. Smartphones are another key component of the digital real estate and mobile use is growing rapidly across the continent.

Smartphones are useful tools that allow for fast communication and can also be used as a learning tool. As more and more smartphones get into the hands of people, greater progress will be made in the digital space as it helps contribute to the pool of knowledge on the internet through content.

The stories shared above are proof that most of the progress in the digital space has been made through the efforts of private citizens offering simple solutions to existing problems. It is therefore important for the government to create an enabling environment to allow entrepreneurs and business people to create solutions more easily.

The solutions from the private sector, at least foundationally, need to be simple and obvious as well as serve a basic need. The nature of the problems being solved determine what scale the business is willing to operate at. We have seen, for instance, the impact of MPesa on multiple markets on the continent which tells you how much of a problem it was to move money around. Similarly, the rapid expansion of Uber across the globe is indicative of the magnitude of the problem it has solved and will continue to solve. Africa needs a lot more solutions like that which address a basic need because that's how maximum scale can be achieved.

These foundational business solutions become the basis upon which other businesses are built. Mobile money for example has created very many offshoot solutions that are dependent on reliable payments in order to function. This shows that the foundational businesses, together with other stakeholders, are able to create an ecosystem of supporting businesses and this will bring more people into the digital world.

Another key asset, probably the most important piece, in this new digital world is the talent or skilled personnel. People have to be brought into the fold and given early exposure to these digital tools so as to make better quality as well as more sustainable solutions. These skills are sharpened through an education which is another big investment that governments need to make in order to prepare its population for the modern, technologically advanced future.

Leadership is also a key part of the puzzle as it is important for there to be clarity of vision within these companies operating in the private sector. Good leadership is about laying out the roadmap ahead and this requires vision and focus that trickles down to the rest of the company.

One thing that this year has taught each of us is that it's important to be adaptable and open to changing circumstances in order to survive. The business environment is experiencing major shifts with different trends becoming the new norm. Office space isn't what it used to be barely a year ago. Working from home has become a staple for most companies and some are considering not resuming back to normal even after the pandemic is contained. Making the relevant adjustments during this period might be the difference between surviving as a company and closing shop.

The business environment is a lot more dynamic now and business leaders need to take advantage of this. This year we have learned that businesses' survival needs more than conventional risk management. It also entails innovation and more particularly, considering moving to new territories such as the digital arena.

I was intrigued by the developments in the digital space in East Africa and share that here to challenge other African regions to take notice and collaborate with these industry leaders.

We no longer go online, we live online. That is the simple truth.

2

THE DIGITAL MIGRATION

NOT TO be confused with digital migration from analogue, my use of the term migration here refers to our having moved from our physical activities to living the bulk of our time in our newly-found digital real estate, navigating issues that are unique to this terrain and benefitting in ways we possibly never could otherwise. There are also challenges that are not found on your street, community or local enterprise.

Yes, we've heard it all before. We're being overtaken by technology. We outsource all cognition to our phones or Google. We shop online and apply for jobs online. We even look for love online.

While some might grumble that the internet is having a negative impact on our lives – our attention spans are shorter, we've forgotten how to multitask, and we're getting less sleep – it's important to remember that the online space also encourages creativity and collaboration. It affords lots of wonderful possibilities and opens doors to previously out-of-reach opportunities.

MASSIVE OPEN ONLINE COURSES

It's with great interest that I've been watching the rise of MOOCs, or Massive Open Online Courses. They've been described as the "iTunes of education", and have been turning traditional education models on their head. As a move to democratize education, MOOCs give free access to quality online education from some of the most famed institutions in the world. If you have an internet connection, you can sign up. Students don't receive credit points or degrees, but can complete an engineering or science course from Yale, Columbia, Stanford, and of course, MIT. With more and more Australian universities signing up to MOOCs each year, it's clear that they're here to stay.

DIGITAL HEALTH CARE

While e-health records haven't necessarily received the best rap as of late due to issues of privacy and data-breaches, digital health care certainly has a lot to offer. Online access to health records could change traditional doctor-patient relationships, as patients are more informed and have better control of their treatments. Healthcare and fitness apps that encourage patients to lead a healthier lifestyle using clinically tried-and-tested methods could save health systems huge sums of money. And remote monitoring technology for high-risk patients could also save millions, as Africa's healthcare system struggles to keep up with the number of patients suffering from chronic disease.

BUSINESS IN THE ONLINE SPACE

Last but not least, the online space opens up many opportunities for businesses who are competing for attention and for customers.

A business that goes online receives instant exposure to a global, ever-growing audience. They can keep their doors open 24/7, and build their brand, their voice and their authority by speaking to more customers in more ways, all the time. It gives the little guys a chance to play on an equal footing with those that are more established.

So while you might feel like switching off and unplugging from time to time, it's important to remember that the internet offers much more than likes, swipes and tweets. It's an ever-expanding online space that's changing every day. It is also where we live, learn, play and connect, daily.

COVID-19 ACCELERATED OUR DIGITAL MIGRATION

Like many people around the world, I expected the months of social distancing to feel, well, distant. But I've been more connected than ever. My inboxes are full of invitations to digital events — Zoom conferences, Skype book clubs, Periscope jam sessions. Strangers and subject-matter experts are sharing relevant and timely information about the virus on social media, and organizing ways to help struggling people and small businesses.

There is no use sugar-coating the virus, which has already had devastating consequences for people all over the world. There have been too many lives lost, businesses closed, and communities thrown into financial hardship. Nobody is arguing that what is coming will be fun, easy or anything remotely approaching normal for a very long time.

But if there is a silver lining in this crisis, it may be that the virus is forcing us to use the internet as it was always meant to be used — to connect with one another, share information and resources, and come up with collective solutions to urgent problems. It's the healthy, humane version of digital culture we usually see only in schmaltzy TV commercials, where everyone is constantly using a smartphone to visit far-flung grandparents and read bedtime stories to kids.

Already, social media seems to have improved, with more reliable information than might have been expected from a global pandemic. And while the ways we're substituting for in-person interaction aren't perfect, we are seeing an explosion of creativity as people try to use technology as a bridge across physical distances.

Today, virtual yoga classes, virtual church services, virtual dinner parties, virtual funerals and baby showers are not the themes of Hollywood movies, they are our reality. These are the kinds of creative digital experiments we need, and they are coming at a time when we need them more than ever.

Covid-19 presented yet another epidemic one of loneliness and isolation brought on by the virus or what is being popularly referred to as the 'social recession'. This recession will hit certain groups especially hard — older people, people with disabilities, people who live alone. But we will all feel isolated to some degree. And as long as it remains unwise to gather in physical spaces, we will need to create virtual spaces that can sustain us.

Building a virtual world to replace a broken physical one is not a new idea. It has been a staple in sci-fi narratives for decades, including classics like "Snow Crash" and "Ready Player One." Many of these stories are dystopian in nature — in them, virtual reality is simply an escape from a real world that is falling apart.

But digital tools can also help strengthen our real-world ties if we use them the right way.

One thing we know for certain is that actively participating in online culture is far better than passively consuming it. Research shows that people who use social media actively — by sending messages, leaving comments or talking in group chats, for example — report being happier than those who simply scroll through their feeds, absorbing news stories and viral videos. Netflix binges and YouTube rabbit holes are fine for escapism, but if you're looking to find solace on the internet, lurking alone won't cut it — you need to contribute.

We also know that not all platforms are created equal. With so much alarming information flying around, private group messages and videoconferences are likely to produce calmer, more nourishing interactions than public platforms like Twitter and Facebook, both of which are designed to amplify content that is outrageous, divisive or otherwise highly engaging.

While the virus forced us indoors, we should be thinking of ways to invest in our digital spaces, and build robust virtual connections that can replace some of the physical proximity we're losing, as well as mobilizing to support our real-world communities in a time of enormous need.

We can use technology to meet this crisis, rather than just distracting ourselves from it. Perhaps after spending years using technologies that mostly seemed to push us apart, the coronavirus crisis is showing us that the internet is still capable of pulling us together.

Your "digital footprint" includes all traces of your online activity, including your comments on news articles, posts on social media, and records of your online purchases. When you know the boundaries of your digital footprint and take steps to contain it, you can help protect your identity and your reputation.
Unknown

3

DIGITAL FOOTPRINT DEFINED

The art of tracking animals involves each and every sign of the animal's presence that can be found in nature, including ground spoor, scent, feeding signs, pellets, visual, auditory and incidental signs. However, footprints are the easiest to identify. They provide the most detailed information on identity, movements and activities of animals and once a trail has been identified, other signs can be studied in more detail. Even where no clear footprints can be found, one can collect bits of information from studying several footprints and piece them together to compile an image of the complete trail.

By the same token, once we establish a trail on the Internet, our footprints give away much about us, our buying habits, what we like to read or study, even down to our idiosyncrasies.

Information and communication technologies have become an integral part of many individuals' day-to-day lives across the planet. The globalization of the world that has been aided by the development of social media platforms and a general inclination to digitalized operations has influenced people to operate through the internet as the new norm. Platforms such as email, messaging, audio calls, video chats, and online messaging rooms have completely changed the terrain of communication in the 21st century. Social institutions such as family, religion, and schools have all changed their approach to connecting with their members. Data transmission is now being done online through the Internet that leaves a trail or pattern of a person's interactions.

Digital footprints can, therefore, be defined as the information or data of a specific individual stored on the internet resulting from online activity. Digital footprints reveal one's behavior, preferences, and social life depending on which websites the individual visits. The internet comprises a bottomless virtual storage system that can hold unparalleled amounts of retrievable data over long periods. Social media platforms' privacy policies often go unnoticed as individuals pay little or no attention to the websites during account opening sessions. The acceptance of website cookies allows the storage of browsing information that may be kept on the computer even when it is switched off.

Because we do not typically pay attention to these polices, we have allowed the Big Data firms to use the information freely as agreeing to the terms and condition gifts them that ability. These companies are able to use the information to understand peoples' needs and preferences and get to use the data to their advantage. For instance, signing up on Facebook grants the application the right to use a person's digital footprint to determine what advertisements are tailored to their buying habits. Things like search results on a specific website can be used to determine an individual's thoughts and needs at different times of the day. Therefore, the website gets to select what information appears on the page on different occasions.

USES OF DIGITAL FOOTPRINTS

Africa's development progress has been steady over the years but not fast enough to catch up with the European giants like United Kingdom and Russia. The continent is still in the developing stages and has faced some challenges in establishing effective digital systems as a result of technological and infrastructural barriers. However, there is still the existence of digital footprints in the websites that are based on the continent. The specific websites have helped companies with an online presence to benefit from the digital footprints of their clients in substantive ways. Prominent online businesses in Africa such as Jumia have been among those that have benefitted the most from the digital footprints of their clients.

Jumia has been among the companies that have been at the forefront of using peoples' digital footprints in customizing the data appearing on their website. The company essentially operates as an online store and has an aggressive advertising system that cuts across other websites and software applications of mobile phones as well computers. The firm can pick data based on one's searches or previous purchases and use it to determine the preferences of purchase of the individual. It is an online corporate move that has proven to be successful in the increase pf sales of given products.

Companies like Twitter and Facebook have also benefitted from the existence of peoples traces on the internet. Twitter being a website that allows different people from different corners of the world to connect uses algorithms to determine and sync individuals with similar patterns. The advantage of such actions is the effortless flourishing and connecting of individuals. The websites ease the building of virtual relations between people who hold just the online knowledge of a person's thoughts. It has become a magnificent way of operation as the website has continued to gain more people signing up on a daily basis. Twitter has also benefitted from ease of forming online friendships that are bolstered by having similar interest derived from the numerous filtering algorithms. Facebook too has taken a similar approach with its marketing, friendship suggestions and data sharing plan.

Online businesses have become increasingly active over the last few decades. People's presence online has also significantly increased given that individuals are becoming more active in connecting through social medial than they previously did. Businesses have discovered that it is easier to reach a larger audience online than on a real-life basis.

The booming of online shops can be exemplified by the existence of Facebook, Instagram and Whatsapp. The social media applications have allowed businesses to connect to larger audiences and therefore make more sales to clients. As a result, delivery businesses have also picked up in an immense manner as the products are moved around to reach the consumers. Fast food companies that offer home delivery services have been at the forefront of online marketing.

Digital footprints allow the consumers to have a select way of operation based on the information fed into the internet. Individuals now have better access to news and other relevant information more closely than before. Paper print media has been as persistent as ever, but digital news is slowly taking larger strides toward becoming the world leading news avenue. Nowadays it is easier to see breaking news via the internet than on television or other media outlets. The direct translation of the matter is that people can access regular information based on their traces. How a person choses to use the information is dependent on their liking and preferences.

Digital footprints have a had both direct and indirect impact on the national performance of the economy. Countries that have high internet activity have enabled their citizens to participate in online businesses and have therefore benefitted from better living standards of the population and higher output of businesses. Digital footprints allow businesses and or individuals to create brands that are followed and respected by the target markets. The business thrives through providing goods and services befitting the needs of the customers and target groups.

TRACKING DIGITAL FOOTPRINTS IN AFRICA

Africa has made fairly decent progress in the transmission and usage online data in the last decade. The introduction of new technologies and improved learning systems has proved to be beneficial in changing the approach to online data. Universities are producing more computer literate individuals than previously seen. The interaction with nationals from developed continents has also enabled the continent to progress towards computer literacy. The introduction of smartphones the subsequent infiltration into the African market has also had a positive impact on their respective economies.

Tracking of digital footprints requires the input of various software that are implanted in the coding of the specific websites in need. One key user of tracking digital footprints is the government security agents responsible for crime prevention. Governments have policies that mandate websites to share data with them regarding the activities of interested persons. Big Data companies also have the necessary tools to use the tracking of digital data of individuals.

It is worth noting that digital data goes beyond a single entity as in some cases it may belong to organizations involving numerous individuals. For instance, countries such as Kenya, South Africa and Tanzania have benefitted from the existence of foreign aid and intelligence from the United Kingdom. The input of foreign personnel and skill has aided in the creating of skill enabling tracking of data transmission relating to crime prevention.

Military intelligence is another area that is reserved in the usage of tracking of digital footprint. Military intelligence relies on online data and proxies transmitted among the masses on a daily basis. The military is responsible for intercepting terror attacks that serve as a threat to democracy and national security. The government therefore gives military units the greenlight to track digital footprints among online sites of businesses, communication, social media as well as many others. It is a niche that has been a beneficial factor and has helped in the securing of many African countries as learned from western and European states.

The question is no longer just what information companies will collect about us, but how this information will be put to use, the ability to transfer it, sell it, conduct marketing experiments with it and base advertising appeals upon it.

4

DIGITAL CAPTURE AND EXPLOITATION

The commercial development of increasingly sophisticated digital media technologies means that one of the key legal and regulatory issues in coming years will be the control and use of information gathered about consumers and citizens as they go about their wired lives.

The same data that can provide leads for potential hires and clients serves treble duty by providing data for targeted marketing appeals, based on a search of keywords in friend profiles, the application makes recommendations of friends who might be interested in the offer, which users can then choose to take action on. The application links data from the social networks of individual employees to a proprietary consumer relationship marketing database to track leads, make follow-up offers, and report on campaign success to see how their viral campaigns stack up to other marketing programs.

The limitations of a privacy-based approach to digital applications are multiple. In the first place, notions of privacy tend to focus on individual rights and personal choice. If an employee 'freely' chooses to use an application that lays their information bare, it is likely to be deemed that it is simply a matter of individual preference.

Why should regulators or other legal authorities intervene? Moreover, applications that are out there can function in ways that ostensibly protect employee privacy – narrowly construed – by delinking marketing and consumer appeals from particular employees, or by ensuring that employers don't have direct access to information about the personal lives of employees. And yet, neither of these claims seems satisfactory.

Even if employees have the 'choice' (at least for the moment) of putting their social networks to use, it seems like a forced one, precisely because the notion of privacy does not take into account the power relations that structure the choice.

Further, even if employers don't have direct access to employee Facebook data, the very notion that this information is transformed into informational capital for the use of third parties remains disturbing. It anticipates a world in which our social contacts become one more asset on the job market, in which the work we put into building and maintaining social relationships becomes instrumentalized, one more standing reserve for the data mine.

At the societal and regulatory level, we need to do more than to argue that individuals have the right to choose whether or not to submit to the forms of monitoring required by access to commercial applications; we need to interrogate why they might be choosing to 'accept' levels of monitoring that they are uncomfortable with. We also need to come up with a theory for explaining why they might have reason to be concerned about monitoring – not just its potential abuses, but also its explicit use for the purpose of targeted forms of marketing and manipulation. Understanding the ways in which power relations might structure access to information resources in the information age and, second, how to describe the forms of exploitation that result are useful in policy decisions.

The Changing Information Landscape

Perhaps as a result of post-Cold War complacency, public concerns over surveillance and monitoring have been at least partially eclipsed by consumers' enthusiastic embrace of the convenience of customization and interactivity provided by online media in particular. The acceptance of the changing information landscape has lead former United Kingdom Information commissioner Richard Thomas to note that we may "sleepwalk into a surveillance society". New technologies and applications including 'smart' phones and social networking sites generate a widening and deepening range of information about consumers. Digital technology makes it possible not only to document the details of the networked citizen's daily lives, but to store, sort, and manage this information.

A term that is widely used in discussions of new media, 'usergenerated content', broadly construed, goes far beyond its common association with the proliferation of Weblogs, personal Web pages, and other forms of amateur media production. It also includes the tremendous amounts of data that consumers generate about themselves when they interact with a new generation of networked digital devices.

Media and cultural studies, long engaged in the study of media audiences, have tended to focus on new manifestations of audience productivity rather than how these audiences are themselves put to work by these proliferating forms of audience monitoring. Scholars and commentators have described the new forms of consumer monitoring in dramatic terms as, "the end of privacy" and the "destruction of privacy." Other scholars have noted, however, that the end of privacy is not an accurate description of an era in which details of personal information are being captured and privatized at an unprecedented level.

Industries that rely on this information have tended to downplay privacy concerns, suggesting that the market is the best way to decide whether consumers are willing to surrender control over their personal information. Such an argument, however, makes two presuppositions that aren't supported by the research: first, that consumers are aware of the extent to which they are surrendering control over personal information and second, that the market has provided them with a meaningful set of choices for control over the collection and use of their personal information.

Public awareness of the extent and character of, for example, online monitoring, lags behind industry practice. Consider a recent survey of residents in the relatively tech-savvy United States' (U.S.) state of California which found, "that a gulf exists between consumers' understanding of online rules and common business practices." The majority of respondents falsely believed that online privacy policies prohibited third-party information sharing and provided them with the rights to delete personal information upon request, sue for damages, and to access and correct data.

In reality, the mere existence of a privacy policy provides no such rights, and so-called privacy policies often stipulate consent to the very practices consumers thought they prohibited. A similar poll conducted by the Annenberg Public Policy Center in the U.S. found, "wide ignorance of business practices and the use of personal information."

The existing state of affairs then, seems to present a paradox. On the one hand surveys continue to reveal the public's high level of concern over privacy; whereas on the other, members of this same public seem increasingly willing to submit to commercial forms of monitoring on a proliferating range of platforms and applications even as they engage in deliberate forms of public self-disclosure from blogging, to public journaling, Tweeting, and updating their personal profiles for a growing group of Facebook 'friends'.

From a commercial perspective the apparent inconsistency is a productive one, since the emerging mass-customized economy relies on detailed portraits of consumer tastes and behaviour to target advertising appeals. The amount of personal information put out there is perfect for marketers. It's an absolute treasure box.

The fact that consumers submit to monitoring while expressing concern over privacy is no more inexplicable than the fact that people work while criticizing exploitative workplace conditions. The choice faced by the public is to submit to monitoring or go without – that is to drop out of a burgeoning online community.

Consumers are entering a world in which access to the goods and services they seek requires willing submission to increasingly detailed forms of data collection and online monitoring. They are faced with a choice that is structured not by their own preferences but by the economic imperatives of the private corporations that have recently come to dominate the internet. The latter aren't choosing to submit to monitoring because they like it; they are exchanging their personal information for access to commercial services.

Marketers defend this logic of exchange in three ways: consumers are freely accepting the terms of exchange when they agree to end-user license agreements, targeted ads are preferable to 'spam', and finally they argue that submission to monitoring is one of the duties of consumers in a commercially supported online economy (there's no such thing as a free lunch, even online).

The term 'enclosure' invokes not just the notion of a space – virtual or otherwise – that is rendered interactive, but also the process of enclosure, whereby places and activities become encompassed by the monitoring embrace of an interactive (virtual) space. Accompanying this movement is a not-so-subtle shift in social relations: entry into the digital enclosure carries with it, in most cases, the condition of surveillance or monitoring.

We can go into a bookstore and make a cash purchase without generating information about the transaction. But when we go online, we generate increasingly detailed forms of transactional information that become secondary information commodities: data that may eventually be sold to third parties or used by marketers for targeted advertising campaigns.

What has been described as the process of digital enclosure might be considered a 'movement' to the extent that the reach of the interactive embrace continues to expand and reconfigure itself. At present, many traditional forms of transaction and interaction can still take place offline: we don't have to buy our books online. But when the local bookstore closes down because it can't keep up with Amazon.com, we may have to.

For many services, however, we do find ourselves reliant upon monitored transactions: interactive digital video recorders, for example, come with submission to monitoring as a built-in condition of use. Cable companies may not be using the data they get from their set-top boxes, but they could.

Internet access requires going through a service provider that can collect and store information about patterns of internet use and online activity. Access to online social networks, like Facebook, entail submission to commercial forms of monitoring. Buying music online is a monitored transaction in a way that a cash purchase in a record store need not be. There is a pattern here: the use of interactive technologies lend themselves to the generation of cybernetic information, feedback about the transactions themselves.

This feedback becomes the property of private companies that can store, aggregate, sort and, in many cases, sell the information in the form of a database or cybernetic commodity to others.

The convenience of the continually-connected society is more than seductive; it provides real benefits. Communicating and purchasing are streamlined and simplified, but we have very little access to the forms of information collection and circulation that are taking place 'behind the scenes'. Companies are able to track our movements, our transactions, and our communications without our permission or, in many cases, knowledge. The unprecedented convenience is enabled by the operation of a network of complex and costly information technology whose increasing functionality is inversely proportional to the typical user's knowledge about how the system works.

Those who live in a wired world know, for example, that shopping has become virtually 'friction-free' – that they can window shop, compare prices and order products without leaving the privacy of home. But they likely have only the vaguest idea about what happens to the information they provide about themselves in the process – their address, product preferences, credit card number, clothing sizes, and so on.

Mobile phone users know that they can remain in constant contact with friends and family, but they might be surprised to know that in some locations, for example, their mobile phones are being used to track traffic patterns, or that the 'pings' sent out by their phone, even when they are not using it, allow their path to be traced throughout the course of the day.

Interactivity is not necessarily a two-way street – more often than not it amounts to the offer of convenience in exchange for willing or unwitting submission to increasingly detailed forms of information gathering. In the end, we need to ask why this might matter.

TALKING OF EXPLOITATION

Much of the celebratory hype over the way in which the internet creates a new generation of audience-producers blurs the important line between access to the means of online content production and ownership or control over these resources. Consumers may own computers and software, but not the networks and vast server farms that make possible the creation and maintenance of online social networks as well as the forms of content sharing that characterize the emerging online economy. Thus, any comparison of industrial-era production to information-age creativity needs to take into account not just the fact that productive resources are in the hands of consumers, but also that the means of communication and distribution are not.

A narrow focus on user-generated content helps to obscure the fact that the privatisation of network infrastructures and the commercialization of online applications lies at the core of emerging online business models. When we explore what people do on social networking sites, for example, and the forms of community such sites enable, we must also keep in mind what is done with the products of this activity, who controls its use and reuse, who profits from its transformation into commercial commodities and marketing campaigns, as well as who is targeted by these campaigns and to what end.

Contrary to conventional wisdom, social networking sites don't publicize community, they privatize it. The same might be said of the whole range of digital platforms onto which increasingly broad swaths of our social, economic, and cultural lives are migrating. We are entering an era characterised by the marriage of unparalleled commercialization with unprecedented monitoring.

Leadership that is focused on our limitations has become irrelevant because we are living in an age in which we must be optimized for possibilities.

5

LEADERSHIP PURE AND SIMPLE

Administering over the transformation of the digital landscape and developing an efficient digital economy posits multiple hurdles for legislative bodies. The basis of these challenges lies in the fact that new competencies are expected from any investments made in digital technologies and big data. In addition, such investments have to be supported with newer skills, institutions, policies and development strategies. Overall, the governing bodies have to expect the transition to new roles. This should ensure that the anticipated dividends from huge technological investments are realized.

First, the state should actively work towards the alignment of new digital age policies to the overall national development strategies. The dynamic nature of technology advancement demands agility in policy creation processes and organizations with a shared philosophy of advancing innovation in future policies. The existence of scale economies and robust networks provide an enabling environment for the eruption of monopolies in the digital platform supply side. Policies should therefore be designed to mitigate such risks and provide an environment that can sustain healthy competition. Specifically, actions should be made towards ensuring universal access to the Internet by making it open, affordable and secure. Moreover, effective regulation and secure market competition should be priority in addition to management of the spectrum and economic scarcity. Transparency of government data, individual data privacy and cybersecurity should also be embedded in state policy.

In contemporary digital life, media is increasingly critical towards the efficient functioning of competitive markets and democracy. State policy in this context works towards the regulation of roles, obligations and responsibilities of content providers and media service in an increasingly multi-platform ecosystem. In the process, the state should enable the creation, aggregation and availability of media content.

In this regard, data protection should be an imperative objective through liaison with stakeholders in the development of policies. Through this, the government can regulate the rights of data subjects and the obligations of data processors and controllers while handling personal data. This also ensures regulation over cross-border data transfers as well as the responsibilities and roles of value chains in data processing.

In order to achieve the promised shared prosperity, governments must control the incremental risks of inequality, control and concentration that are inherent. In the absence of an enabling and competitive environment, the scale economies resulting from digital platforms and the Internet could produce unhealthy monopolies and extreme concentration.

In addition, without proper employee skill development in an increasingly automated work space, inequalities are bound to escalate. Lack of accountability by the government could also lead to greater control over citizen inclusion and empowerment despite the reduction of information scarcity resulting from the advancement of digital technologies. Such risks can only be mitigated through complementary policy reforms in the analogue sectors. Moreover, policies in the digital sectors must reform the socio-economic contexts in which the new technologies are implemented.

Currently, there are concerns over the increasing policy challenges in privacy and security resulting from social media, Big Data and employment hurdles as a result of robotics and artificial intelligence demand organic policies. Moore's law's exponential technology change merged with scale effects present a daunting challenge to policy makers. Due to their complexities, multi-stakeholder involvement is crucial in order to adequately anticipate the overall impact while at the same time reflecting the priorities and values of the society. Therefore, the government should ensure that the national digital initiatives are congruent with the overall national development policies. Such a task demands collaborative communication, strategy management and coordination among the technical ministries and core policy making bodies that are responsible for the digital economy.

Ministries leading macroeconomic management finance and national development strategy must familiarize with the essentials of the digital economy whereas the technical ministries presiding over education and innovation should engage with all stakeholders across the creative process of exploiting digital technologies for sustainable and inclusive development. Contrastingly, education and consensus making can also spur from below as is evident in Finland.

Secondly, the state policies should support research and development while playing an entrepreneurial role in testing and researching speculative technologies and digital platforms. The research should also focus on the human complements to the new technologies and the adaptation and integration with the local context. In practical terms, the research and development will involve monitoring the global patterns and trends and adopting the already successful ones. Afterwards, considerable efforts will be made towards testing and adopting them within the local context prior to scaling activities. It is imperative to assert that the digital technology revolution possesses the widest scope and dynamic growth in human history.

Therefore, an innovative, activist and speculative state should encourage the acquisition of emerging technologies, promote the early adopters of these technologies, and formulate complementary laws and create test apparatus for efficient localization and absorption, as is the case in China.

Third, the state should broaden the backbone telecommunications infrastructure and ensure that the access to the Internet is both affordable and inclusive. National policies on broadband aim to catalyze the installation of broadband infrastructure within a geospatial zone. These policies often specify the ambition with regard to the expected access speeds, time usage during roll out of the service plan, and adoption of the service. In most cases, they are also inclusive of public-private cooperative mechanisms alongside public funding.

The role of the state in this context is to provide an elaborate nation-level pivot for stakeholder engagement. In addition, the state must guard consumer and national interests, experimenting with measures before nation-wide adoption, promoting the use of broadband, creating a clearinghouse for viably efficient projects, and carrying out monitoring and evaluation.

Achieving success in broadband diffusion demands channeling attention to demand and supply side issues as evidenced in developed countries. Policies aimed at the supply side are tailored towards promoting networking infrastructure whereas demand side policies aim to promote overall adoption and increased awareness of services. A nation-wide approach would require the use of multiple strategies in order to achieve national build-out of broadband networks. These approaches vary by the nature of local circumstances, although some may be universally applicable.

In reality, the private sector is charged as the primary driver of the development of broadband in the majority of countries. In developed countries, most of the private companies are locally founded, whereas less developed states rely mostly on foreign direct investments. In the latter case, appropriate incentives are crucial and in addition to clear legal and regulatory environments and feasible development plans should make up the broadband strategies. In order to accelerate high deployment rates of infrastructure and competition, governments in such cases may be enticed to require the sharing of infrastructure.

To counter problems related to connectivity in the short to medium term, governments have tried and used several methods. One of these is through the implementation of special incentives and policies that attract infrastructure development in rural areas. Another common method is the subsidizing of networks for a collection of grouped users whose ability to connect to the networks is critical for the development of the economy and society. Examples include academic, government, research and development and educational institutions.

For social welfare reasons, some governments have enforced shared access of ICT tools and the Internet for areas with disadvantages. An example of this case is evident in Brazil where the government works alongside civil society, local entrepreneurs and private operators to fill the existing accessibility gaps experienced by the poor communities based in rural regions.

Fourth, the national governments should invest heavily in human capital and complements to organizations through institutional learning spanning across all sectors of the economy in order to secure inclusion and the realization of digital dividends. Substantial investment should ensure organizational changes, innovation of processes and other intangible assets like digital content and data. Such capabilities require significant shifts in roles, routines, skills, cross-sector partnerships, teamwork, managerial practices and leadership.

The state can play crucial roles in ensuring the effective and wide diffusion of digital technologies through liaisons with relevant stakeholders in poor communities and lagging sectors. State support programs for the adoption of new digital technologies and business practices transformation should be provided for small and medium enterprises (SMEs). This is because SMEs face significant risks, management of change, learning, and capability development during the technology adoption process. OECD countries have been using such programs for their SMEs that include the creation of markets for business development services and industrial extension services.

In the absence of state intervention, digital inequalities will expand which will further reinforce socio-economic inequalities among and within countries. To counter this, the state should provide affordable access to ICT tools, the Internet, digital literacy incentives, and supporting the development of local content, grassroots innovation networks, complementary skills, and informational capabilities. However, absolute eradication of poverty and ensuring inclusivity is not primarily a technological challenge.

These challenges require a greater understanding of the nature of the poor by observing and analyzing their context, their difficulties, their resources, and the amount and quality of information they can access. Capacity building of grassroots organizations and local information intermediaries is required for this task as well as experimenting and piloting. In leading efforts to bridge the observed disparities, the state must collaborate with community organizations, business associations, local government, civil society, philanthropic organizations and universities.

The state's mandate of making a more responsive and capable public sector, enhancing accountability, policy making, and enhancing citizen participation should be achieved through leveraging of the digital revolution. Currently, there is no other option than to embark on digital transformation of all governments and their services. This is because all current governments face a complex combination of challenges that include rising citizen expectations with regards to public service delivery; escalating budget constraints; widening inequalities in incomes, opportunities and access; increasing calls for better accountability and transparency; falling public trust on account of undelivered past promises; and the competitive need to adapt to a dynamic and knowledge based global economy.

In order to achieve this transformation, the government should revisit its relationship with its citizens and adopt a more customer-centric approach in its dealings. This is comparative to the introduction of a disruptive technology into an archaic system. It demands an absolute paradigm shift in the overall perspectives. The government should provide services in a manner that makes sense to the rational client. This goes against the conventional approach by the government that is focused on agency in charge of service delivery.

All complementing variables such as payment mechanisms, timing, procedures and service levels are all constructed around this agency approach. On the other hand, a customer-centric approach replaces the agency with the citizen, meaning that the government services should be available any time the citizen demands them in whatever location and using whatever medium that the citizen sees fit. This is an approach that is proving successful in the United Kingdom, Canada and Singapore in their digital government programs.

As with many other transitive processes, the transformation journey should start with the development of a motivational vision of a desirable government in the future. These visions should encompass the best practices in public sector agency reforms such as placing citizen wants at the center, employing results-based management practices, and service delivery on demand.

They should inherently reflect the citizen aspirations for accountable, transparent and participatory government and should be well communicated to all the relevant stakeholders. Clear accountabilities and broad mobilization for public service performance to citizens are critical for mitigation of emergent resistance from existing organized groups that would not want to change the status quo.

A thought-out investment in e-government combined with civil service reform could have the biggest impact in the future. Digital government in this context refers to the introduction of digitally empowered process reengineering and the transformation of incentives, culture, and skills of the civil service to encourage an environment of collaboration, professionalism, transparency, and accountability. The investment should ensure extensive transformation of routines, power relations and organizations, which means it would be a long-term project that can only materialize under the guidance of a shared, motivating and clear vision.

Deep-rooted shifts in the functionality of the government have been conventionally complex feats. To realize them, the hierarchical, closed, inward-oriented, and closed system have to be turned to decentralized, connected, and service-oriented organizations that can clearly not be achieved by technology on its own. Organizational culture, skills, attitudes, and static routines have to be altered.

Achieving efficiency in digital policy would require proper sequencing and prioritization of a catalogue of e-government tasks that must be steered by a new approach to information sharing and digitization. Complementary public sector reforms must follow suite and stakeholder aligned incentives can catalyze the momentum necessary for entrenched learning and commitment to mitigate the barriers to change where necessary.

Changes in social sectors such as health and education with regards to digital transformation are consistent with the specific changes required to change the whole of government. Fundamentals of such change include leadership and competencies to adapt to transformational change, envisioning a common vision for the future of the specific sectors, mobilization of demand and education programs for consumers, support to policy reforms in sectors, continuous performance evaluation in terms of service delivery and systematic handling with existing gaps in the digital ecosystem of the target sector. In this regard, the government undertakes the two roles of shaping interactions among the components of the digital transform environment and the actors through efficient policy formulation and acting as a market enabler while also serving as a strategic investor in digital technology data and applications that support the evolution of the target sector.

As is the case with nation-wide transformation, the alignment of sectoral incentives and policies with digital transformation incentives is critical to realize the potential for digital transformation of a sector. Such complementary policies are different for every sector. For social sectors such as health and education, key policy reform areas include matters related to accountability, leadership, and effective governance coupled with active citizen participation and manageable demand. It is the duty of the state to align these matters with policy and invest heavily in managing each one.

For private sector-oriented services such as business and financial services, policies must cover competition, skilled labor, regulation, industrial organization, and competition. In this regard, the state serves as an enabler and facilitator. The nation-wide approach is oriented towards contextual intervention and consistent incentives. Inadequate and inefficient state leadership in the pursuit of effective complementary reforms alongside sectorial digital transformation is expected to result in unsustainable or stunted transformation over and above the wasted digital investment.

Emergent state institutions with new capabilities are required to construct and implement a harmonious national digital transformation strategy and policy. Such capabilities are incrementally critical in order to mobilize a long-term commitment to digital transformation, engender a shared vision, and ensure proper proliferation of ICT investments and opportunities into regional, sectorial, and national development strategies. Through private-public-partnerships, the government may acquire enough resources to invest in broadband infrastructure and shared digital platforms.

It is the state's responsibility to set fast-paced reforms in policy, pursue unions with the private sector and civil society, engage stakeholders, establish wide access to digital technology tools and the Internet, and support initiatives that start from the bottom, social learning, and local adaptation. This merger between the old and new roles calls for changes in competencies within the public sector domain and for unions with the civil society and private sector.

Membership to the Digital World Order is free and may see the greatest levelling of the playing field if Africa's leadership and populace awakens to it!
Alan Mwangi

6

LEADING IN THE DIGITAL ERA

DIGITALIZATION HAS completely revamped the competitive business environment through its huge impact on distribution channels, market structures, players, and customer relations. This has made it imperative for organizations to adopt an apex-level strategic perspective on digital transformation.

CEOs have been tasked with new roles and responsibilities to drive the selection and adoption of digital technologies that should drive their organizations' abilities to remain competitive in an increasingly digitalized world. As such, contemporary leaders serve the emergent role of digital enablers and change agents, which implies that they should possess the oversight to identify opportunities posited by emergent technology and then radically push for their implementation. Not only do they play a role in appropriating the best technology for their organizations but also confer a positive mindset to their employees regarding the adoption of new technology. It is their responsibility to instill a digital culture into the lead management teams through ensuring their active involvement in sustainable change.

As such, the need for deeper interaction with the Chief Information Officer is an increasingly important aspect of digital strategy definition and implementation, rather than heaping all the responsibility to the IT leads. In order to achieve their goals, the CEOs have to paint a clear picture of the organizational needs and the qualities of the digital strategies that satisfy these needs.

Contemporary literature has increasingly found interest in the skills that characterize efficient leaders in the digital era. Scholars, in line with contingency and universal theories, analyze the degree of skills that are necessary to lead e-businesses as opposed to the traditional organizational leadership skills. A general consensus is that the introduction of digital tools impacts how work is designed, and specifically how people interact together. For instance, digitalization allows new opportunities such as smart working and virtual teams, new communication tools, faster access to information and speed, increased standardization and efficiency, and effects on power structures. To realize the dividends of digital transformation, effective leaders must possess specific skills that will be analyzed below.

HIGH SPEED DECISION MAKING

One of the biggest impacts of technology has been the change in speed of work. For leaders in this digital era, decisions have to be made more rapidly, implying that decisiveness and problem-solving skills should feature more prominently in future. Incessant urgency means that more often leaders will be required to make decisions even without access to all the information or time required to properly analyze the issue at hand. The risk of relapse to habitual response mechanisms as opposed to the creation of innovative and novel ideas is therefore increased.

To mitigate this risk, leaders are required to breed tolerance to ambiguity while maintaining a high level of creativity. Despite the fact that the new digital world forces leaders to increase their response speed to problems, it also allows them to make more informed decisions due to the availability of real-time data. As a result of this, the ability to process large amounts of big data with the aim of analysis and prioritization of important information for purposes of decision making has become extremely relevant in a rapidly changing world.

It is expected that leaders will have to invest in their relationships with their IT managers and provide them with instructions for data analysis and production of meaningful interpretations.

MANAGING CONNECTIVITY

Traditionally, leaders were expected to create networks for the purpose of stakeholder support and resource acquisition. Modern leaders are expected to foster social interactions with the aim of supporting innovation in all areas. Innovation is increasingly becoming a top priority and leaders must learn to exploit the emergent networking opportunities.

The new hyper-connected environment characterized by the ubiquitous use of social media and other digital platforms, in which e-leaders operate, provide new networking opportunities owing to the ease of accessibility and the coagulation of target groups in a manner that allows immediate communication.

Emergent technologies have reinforced the notion of compulsory participation in the network in light of the growth of social media usage. However, care should be taken in order to realize tangible benefits as opposed to only networking for the sake of it.

MANAGING DISRUPTIVE CHANGE

The rapid and dynamic pace of technological evolution tests the organization's ability to react to continuously evolving situation and players. Modern organizations have to foresee opportunities, adapt, and improvise to maintain their competitive advantages.

Under the weight of incremental pressure to innovate processes, efficient leaders must radicalize their role in identifying and understanding the need for change, in addition to handling and imitating the change to within their team and organizational clusters.

In comparison to traditional leaders, e-leaders must possess higher entrepreneurial desire and a more speculative approach to risk. Caution should be taken in consideration so as to preserve the mission and focus of the organization in light of such disruptive change.

This means that leaders must clarify a common direction while supporting flexibility and innovative attitude in the organization. Therefore, their biggest obstacle in this context lies in their ability to share a common vision about the future and inspire the organization to a new position.

COMMUNICATING THROUGH DIGITAL MEDIA

E-businesses are required to deal with discontinuous and rapid shifts in technology, competition, and demand owing to the fast exchange of information and global connectivity that have made the business environment more competitive and turbulent. The need for speed, accessibility of information, and higher flexibility have necessitated the adoption of more decentralized organizational structures.

Due to the ease and speed of sharing of information and knowledge, followers have gained a higher degree of autonomy whereby they can express themselves across all layers of the organization.

Leaders are also expected to serve as the source of motivation and inspiration for followers implying that these skills have gained significant importance. Through the acquisition of these skills, leaders are able to encourage active participation and involvement of followers. Ironically, the same digital tools that accord followers with higher degrees of autonomy may also be responsible for heightened isolation.

There is an increasing concern over increased isolation of workers, poor accountability, and weaker social bonding. Leaders must therefore help and support their followers to deal with the challenges of increased job demands and greater autonomy through the adoption of coaching strategies that provide resources, promote individual development, assist them in completing their tasks.

In addition, the leader must actively develop a positive organizational environment that encourages higher degrees of unity and collaboration among the employees. In the digital era context, the conventional social skills such as emotional understanding and active listening may no longer be sufficient to the creation of such environments.

To breed tangible outcomes, leaders need to integrate these social skills with the capacity to master a myriad virtual communication tools and methods. This can be termed as e-communication which means the ability to communicate using ICT in way that is organized and clear, avoids miscommunication and errors, and is not detrimental to performance nor is it excessive.

Tone and arrangement of messages should be heavily considered as well as the choice of communication tools or medium. This ability enables the adaptation of the communication to the preferences of the receiver, like in a face-to-face scenario, in order to produce cues necessary for social bonding.

DEVELOPING TECHNICAL SKILLS

In conventional leadership trends, leaders were merely required to have extensive understanding of social intelligence and emotional competencies in order to understand, manage, and motivate teams. However, digital transformation has made it more important for them to understand and manage the use of various technologies.

Knowledge and skills in IT have become essential skills in the operation within a digitalized environment. The mastery of current technologies must be leveled against the ability to foresee the changes in technology and adapt to them as they emerge. Therefore, e-leaders must adopt a life-long learning approach in the context of digital skills.

LEADERSHIP SKILLS IN THE DIGITAL ERA

As already highlighted, an efficient leader in the era of digital transformation must possess a technical mindset and a people orientation. These skills represent different profiles of people that must come together to implement an effective transformation of the organization. As such, there needs to be a lucrative exchange relationship between people-oriented leaders such as sales managers and IT functions so as to make a cross-skill and cross-functional integration.

Systemic dissemination of knowledge from an individual to the group is depicted as the most effective way to disperse expertise and knowledge across the entire organization. This integration can be achieved through reverse-mentoring initiatives. However, a problem persists owing to generational disparities where the newer generations with more skill and knowledge in digital technologies may concentrate informational power over older generations, which becomes a source of skepticism and aversion to change.

A source of leadership inspiration is in the modern military operational environments where leaders must lead under uncertain, complex, and volatile circumstances. Leadership training must therefore combine change and technology through the creation of simulations of specific scenarios where improvisation and ambiguous information create complexities and uncertainty. One way to achieve this is through virtual spaces.

In massive community games, team leaders are required to motivate, recruit, retrain, and reward the talented members of the team. As such, they must be ready to make quick decisions that profoundly affect the long-run outcomes whereby they must analyze their environments so as to keep their competitive advantage. Simulations therefore provide a possibility to exercise learning in situations that would have otherwise been impossible.

In addition, higher participation is more achievable since the digital transformation enables real-time contribution by followers in many decision-making processes. Therefore, leaders are expected to undertake a more inclusive style of governance that involves looking into the ideas of followers in routine decision-making by using two-way interaction and communication. The higher levels of autonomy experienced by the followers instill a greater sense of responsibility for their administered tasks.

As in any market, there will be losers and winners—some of which are already emerging.

7

CHALLENGES AND OPPORTUNITIES

LET ME start by defining the Africa we are talking about. Perhaps that will pinpoint the massive opportunities inherent on the continent on the one hand, and the incredulous challenges that exist. However, we do know that the greatest achievers are those that took on a challenge and turned it around into the greatest opportunity. We already saw that with M-Pesa, Sweep South and Uber, among others.

In order to have any impact on any African nation, region or the continent as a whole, it is important to understand the continent's bewildering scale and complexity. Africa's land area exceeds that of China, Europe, and the United States combined. Its 54 countries have a collective population of 1.2 billion. It has over a thousand languages and huge diversity in income levels, resource endowment, infrastructure development, educational attainment, and business sophistication.

Without any doubt, there is a lot to gain for African countries through the incorporation of digital technology in national development drives. Although Africa historically lagged, this young continent, with a median age of around 20, has become an eager adopter and innovator in all things digital and mobile. There are already 122 million active users of mobile financial services in Africa. The number of smartphone connections is forecast to double from 315 million in 2015 to 636 million in 2022—twice the projected number in North America and not far from the total in Europe. Over the same period, mobile data traffic across Africa is expected to increase sevenfold.

I pause here to point out an opportunity that African governments totally missed and that must be a lesson going forward. In the early 1990s as the cell phone industry was still a budding phenomenon; governments had the opportunity to tap into that gravy train. However, given the myopic lenses most governments see their citizenry through, they tried the control approach. In no time, they were overtaken by the savvy entrepreneurs and have never caught up. This has made most government-run telecommunications entities almost obsolete. Perhaps it is a lesson that governments should stick to provide an enabling environment for their populace to run industry.

It is in the same manner that banks underestimated the segment of society that does not check all the boxes. Many were underbanked while others were unbanked. Voila, a new player enters the market on a digital pathway, M-Pesa, and the rest is history but a history with many casualties for those who did not embark on the digital journey at the right time.

It is definitely not gloom for developing nations as there are a number of emergent opportunities that countries can exploit to remain competitive in the digital era. One of the most successful is the digitization of retail payment schemes. In Kenya, digital payment systems for most government and business services, has resulted in the revolution of the entire retail payment structure of the country. Like other economies exploiting this revolution, billions of dollars are saved annually through the use and centralization of electronic payments. It is by far the youngest beneficiary of the cell phone-based transaction and payment platforms and it has experienced several incredible advantages. This is especially significant in developing countries as it cuts across all social classes and sectors.

With this observation, it would be in the best interest of African countries to join the Better Than Cash Initiative (BTCA), a global partnership program that promotes the use of digital payments over cash. It also supports the development of payments infrastructure with the objective of centralizing government payments and transactions in an electronic system. As a result, the economies will benefit from these developments.

Digitization should also provide opportunities for financial inclusion of the marginalized populations and female financial empowerment. Previous hindrances to financial access such as minimum balance requirements, geographical barriers to access financial institutions, low credit issues, and inconsistent and low income flows can now be circumvented. Micro savers now have the opportunity to operate bank accounts, savings have increased, and financial institutions can now safely offer reasonably priced short-term credit.

In the last five years there have been 20 million virtual bank savings accounts opened compared to the existing 30 million deposit accounts in the entire banking sector of Africa. Therefore, digitization has made financial access possible while also creating access to markets. The entry point has been through the telecommunications sector that is versatile enough in its range of productivity and its replicability across countries.

Virtual savings and credit platforms allow users to better manage their inconsistent cash flows, apply for quick loans, and cope with uncertainty of needs. This unique combination lessens the savings to investments cycle for the low-income earners and creates links for financial inclusion, sustainable poverty reduction, and inclusive growth. Inclusion in this context therefore becomes the enabler of development rather than an end, a promoter of individual progress, and a powerful conduit through which sustainable development goals are achieved.

Countries that have embraced digital financial inclusion have seen dramatic eruption of strong banks as more citizens open new bank accounts. The increased demand deposit accounts have allowed these banks to innovate and intermediate savings. In addition, the high volumes of transactions have attracted new entrants into the financial markets that bring new innovative ideas and much needed capital to fuel the local economies.

Finally, the ripple effect from financial inclusion has a strong linkage to more effective monetary policy frameworks. In East Africa, the decline of currency outside the banking sector owing to innovations in the financial system allows for more product introduction and new players provide important signals for monetary policy action. In East Africa, mobile money is used as frequently as paper money and therefore, the region accounts for four-fifths of the world's transactions. With text messages it is possible to send money to another mobile that can be cashed out of the system using tens of thousands of participating agents. It is estimated that half of Kenya's GDP moves through mobile money, mostly using the pioneering service M-Pesa, which has some 14 million users.

By the same token, technology has changed the traditional labor models in many countries. Nowadays, it is quite common for consumers to sell products to other consumers at an international scale, implying that they serve the role of a producer simultaneously. This is achieved through the sale of personal items using online market platforms such as eBay and Amazon. Services are also marketed and sold using online platforms such as Airbnb and Uber.

Through peer-to-peer exchanges facilitated by the Internet, shared economies are able to utilize the untapped resources through increasing the accessibility of shared services and goods. This creates a new sector that generates additional opportunities for revenue. They therefore bridge the gap between formal and informal sectors and in turn raises the level of participation.

International outsourcing has allowed previously unutilized potential to take advantage of shifting skill demands for the future. Knowledge and skills are transferred in the process and governments are able to capture new avenues of income that were previously non-existent. Governments now have easier monitoring of activities and transactions, which should in turn assist in countering run-away money laundering and corruption.

I will not pretend that Africa is an easy place to do business, given its geographic complexity, infrastructure gaps, and relative economic and political volatility. However, I believe it is the most lucrative digital landscape in which to plant your entrepreneurial seeds. In short, Africa is a 1.2 billion–person market on the cusp of transformative growth. It already has more big companies than you would imagine—but room for many more. And most excitingly, an entrepreneurial energy pulses throughout the continent.

However, for leaders seeking to prosper with business in Africa, it starts with mapping a clear-eyed strategy, but that's far from sufficient. Pursuing business-model innovation, unleashing local talent, building long-term resilience, and promoting local development also are "must dos" in Africa. In the closing chapter of this book I share with you Africa's priorities through the eyes of a number African leaders, each of whose journey helps illustrate crucial aspects of this framework for growth.

Africa is grasping the technological revolution with both hands. Hundreds of millions of venture capital dollars are flowing into the region which remains the fastest growing mobile phone market in the world, and an emerging competitor in the global race for tech.

With innovation hubs sprouting up throughout the continent, solutions are being found to solve uniquely African problems and dissolve barriers to trade, financial services and capital. But governments need to do more to seize on the opportunities of the global digital economy, which is set to grow from $11.5 trillion in 2016 to over $23 trillion by 2025.

In response, the UN Economic Commission for Africa (ECA) set the focus of its 2019 conference of African ministers of finance, planning and economic development squarely on the subject.

Held in Marrakesh in March under the title *"Fiscal Policy, Trade and the Private Sector in the Digital Era: A Strategy for Africa"*, the conference was chaired by Morocco's secretary general of the Ministry of Finance, Zouhair Chorfi, who introduced it saying, *"Digitalization is a great opportunity for Africa. It can transform Africa by increasing competitiveness, promoting strong integration, and reducing the cost of doing business."*

The digital economy already accounts for more than 5% of gross domestic product (GDP) in some African nations. This could be more than doubled to 12-20% if countries harness the economic potential of digital technology.

The ability of countries to do this will determine how fast they grow in the coming decade, and will help them raise up to $400bn to bridge their $600bn financing gap.

Africa shows every sign of being ready for rapid economic transformation in the coming decade, but countries need to digitize their economies and reform their tax systems to drive revenues and finance development, said ECA executive secretary Vera Songwe in her opening speech.

"The importance of digitalization and the digital economy in driving growth and structural transformation, as well as optimizing fiscal performance in Africa cannot be overstated," she said. *"Such digital developments can have a transformative effect across the economy by reducing barriers to entry and expanding market reach for businesses, creating jobs, and boosting both domestic and foreign trade in goods and services."*

The continent's burgeoning populations and embryonic levels of technology and underdeveloped infrastructure can be turned to an advantage if countries adopt new technologies straight away and use them to leapfrog into the 21st century.

Master the Digital Future of Industry and increase your Competitive advantage. Whatever you do, don't get left behind.

8

THE DIGITAL TRANSFORMATION JOURNEY

IN THIS rapidly changing landscape, there is a need for leaders in commerce who are able and willing to enable modernization of their business strategy by bringing Digital Transformation and technology together. From creating a digital-first mind-set, helping to re-imagine business and business models, to making sure that everyone and everything is connected. Those that are designing Digital Transformation journeys that create meaningful impact for their business will emerge as industry leaders. The leadership that I am talking about goes beyond the company one is leading to the entire industry.

A quick look across Africa gives one the impression that many companies are not sufficiently bold in the magnitude and scope of their digital investments. Two pathways exist depending on where businesses find themselves on their digitization journey.

The "disruptors"—those that initiate digital disruptions—receive the biggest payouts, whereas the "fastfollowers"— those with operational excellence and superior organizational health—are not far behind.

It seems to me that, on average, many companies and indeed, entire industries have made little progress in their efforts to digitize their business models. Those that have made strong gains from digitization have followed either the disruptor or the fast-follower model.

It's safe to say that the landscape in South Africa is no different. Many of South Africa's large corporates, outside of banking, high tech, and telecommunications, which sit ahead of the pack, are in the early stages of their digitization journey. From the mining and chemical industries to retail, many traditional businesses are only just beginning to implement digital strategies.

One of the biggest differentiating factors between the top economic performers and others is how quick and adaptable they are in setting, executing, and adjusting their digital strategies. There is much discussion across all industries about the various ways to speed up digital delivery and drive closer alignment between business and IT in South Africa. While most organizations are in the early stages of implementing agile at scale, financial-services firms lead the charge. Although few companies can mount disruptive strategies at the ecosystem level in the same way as Alibaba, Amazon, Google, and Tencent, which have radically pushed digitization on their respective platforms, some are doing this well. For instance, South African insurer Discovery is at the forefront of ecosystem thinking with its Vitality platform. Today, millions of users track their health using Vitality and participate in activities to earn loyalty points with Discovery's extensive network of partners, including British Airways, Emirates, and Europcar. By partnering with local providers, the insurer was able to penetrate international markets.

Leadership in this space requires that investments are made in the right assets and as I alluded to earlier, one of Africa's greatest assets aside from its minerals, agricultural land, water, and excellent weather in large parts of the continent, is tis youth. Not just its youth but a generation of young people who are vibrant, hungry for adventure and creative into the bargain.

INVEST DIGITAL TALENT AHEAD OF PEERS

A correlation exists between the pace of technological change and the availability of talent to deploy and manage such change. A lack of digital talent is a significant constraint on digital reinvention in South Africa.

Companies like BCX, Cisco, Google, and Microsoft have made headlines for their investment in digital capability building in South Africa. Cisco, for example, invests in the development of the advanced information and communications technology (ICT) talent pool through its networking academy, and BCX has announced a partnership with the Cape Innovation and Technology Initiative to grow scarce digital skills in ICT infrastructure and software programming, cybersecurity, fintech and artificial intelligence.

Elsewhere, Andela, one of Nigeria's best-known start-ups, continues to attract big-ticket funding thanks to its business model of providing companies with outsourced engineering teams. Meeting the demand of South African business will require many more such initiatives, however.

Private-sector partnerships or scalable service providers that mirror the Andela business model, for example, would help to drive talent development at scale and power the digital economy.

Every CEO in South Africa accepts the impact digitization can have, yet few companies have taken concrete steps to turn rhetoric into reality. Those who execute dynamic strategies by building and participating in ecosystems and investing in talent and capabilities early and aggressively, will reap benefits from increased profits but most likely as recognition as industry leaders.

Africa offers exciting opportunities to build large, profitable businesses. Its population is young, fast-growing, and increasingly urbanized—while rapid technology adoption makes the continent a fertile arena for innovation. But Africa's business environment remains poorly understood and known too many executives in the West only by its reputation for complexity, conflict, and corruption.

9

PIONEERING A NEW FRONTIER

A NEW world awaits those willing to discover it. I have always been inspired by the words of University of Kansas Chancellor E.H. Lindley, who in the early 20th century encouraged students to *'develop the spirit of the old pioneers who were not afraid of new problems.'* I also draw inspiration from James E. Faust, who admonished his listeners to *'become pioneers of the future with all its exciting opportunities'*.

As Africa stands at the entrance of the digital era, its leadership must keep in mind that the world was built by people who were not afraid to take risks. They were the pioneers who were not afraid of the wilderness, the scientists who were not afraid of progress, the politicians who were not afraid to challenge the status quo, the slaves who were no afraid of dying, the youth who were not afraid of asking, "Why?" or "Why not? And the dreamers who were not afraid to take action.

The indisputable fact is that the digital age belongs to the youth and Africa's greatest asset is, indeed, its youth. The digital age calls for great imagination and creativity. It calls for innovation and innovation is driven by necessity. Most of the greatest advancements in the digital space have come about as a result of solutions to a problem. Well, Africa has, seemingly, endless problems and there lies the opportunity.

As more and more young people seek meaningful solutions to age-old problems through digital applications (Apps) the digital real estate will continue to expand.

T.S. Eliot said, *"Only those who will risk going too far can possibly find out how far one can go."* You cannot live an extraordinary life by remaining ordinary. It takes faith, courage, and grit to break cultural molds, political and social limitations and family expectations.

A young friend of mine was in law school when, to help out a friend, he started creating content. He turned out to be very good at it and eventually signed up as a freelancer on a particular website. Within a semester, he was earning enough money for his upkeep. Even before he graduated, he was headhunted by an international company which offered him a position as senior content developer. Needless to say, he did not even seek admission to the Bar nor to the law society.

Instead, he took all available Google certifications, continued to create content that was word class. He tells me that during the lockdown he was getting job offers at senior management level when his peers in the legal field were sitting at home, worried whether their jobs would still be there when lockdown was lifted.

Now I am not advocating that anyone who leave their chosen profession; I am just showing how following a vision led my young friend to his destination faster than if he had stayed on the traditional route. He was blessed to have parents who were open-minded and who encouraged him to follow his vision. He recalls his dad saying to him from an early age, *"Learn to be the kind of visionary that raises the bar and levels up the people around him. Dare to join the ranks of those who push humanity forward."*

In order to do what I do effectively, I am a student of people and personalities. There are leaders and there are those who lead. Leaders hold a position of power and influence. Those who lead inspire us

Be it individuals or organizations, we follow those who lead not because we have to, but because we want to. We follow those who lead not for them, but for ourselves. It is my sincere hope that in this digital premise, there will be many who inspire others and many more who want to find someone to inspire them.

One might ask why some people and organizations are more inventive, pioneering and successful than others. And why are they able to repeat their success again and again? In my experience, the answer lies in the fact that in business it doesn't matter what you do, it matters why you do it.

If the older generation that is in political positions are to lead in this era, they must get acquainted with the new terrain and understand what it will take for them to be relevant. Alternatively, they will find themselves sidelined by the more effective players in that field.

On the other hand, I challenge young people to get into the political arena but to refrain from singing the same tunes that are being sung by the old guard. There is an African proverb which says that when the drumbeat changes, the dancers must change their dance steps. The drumbeats have already changed, and if we continue dancing as the old leaders led, we will certainly find ourselves out of step with the best in the world.

There is no question in my mind that if companies in African countries embrace digital, they could outpace their peers and see an increase in profitability and revenue growth. The case for digital reinvention across all industries and sectors has been clear for some years: companies that embrace digital will outpace their peers financially and benefit from greater profitability and higher revenue growth.

The pace of change, however, is slow. Research published by a reputable research and management company in 2017 showed that, despite the apparent ubiquity of digital technologies in day-to-day life, industries were less than 40 percent digitized on average. Even with relatively deep penetration of technology in media, retail, and high tech, traditional industries contributed to the lag and continue to do so today.

Africa offers growth-minded companies exciting opportunities. Its population is young, fast growing, and increasingly urbanized. The rapid adoption of technology, meanwhile, makes the continent a fertile arena for innovation.

10

LESSONS FROM AFRICA'S
EMINENT LEADERS

IN AFRICAN tradition, a story almost always ends with the lesson. The lesson is spiced with examples. I will therefore stay true to tradition and share with you some priorities as seen through the eyes of several African leaders who have raised the bar in business.

JAMES MWANGI: EQUITY BANK, KENYA

James Mwangi, CEO of Kenya-based Equity Bank, built the company with one core purpose in mind: to solve the social problem of lack of access to financial services. Equity Bank was born out of Mwangi's turnaround of a then-small Kenyan building society, which was converted into a commercial bank in 2004. Today, it has more than 12 million clients in six countries across East and Central Africa, as well as nearly $5 billion in assets and reported pre-tax profits of $270 million.

James Mwangi: I grew up in a rural area of Kenya, and my own mother, Grace, didn't have a bank account. The nearest bank branch was 50 kilometers away, and the minimum opening balance was equivalent to several years of her earnings. My mother would also have been intimidated by banks, with their granite floors, long queues, and formally dressed officials.

To make matters worse, banks often had a seven-day rule between withdrawals. If your child got sick, you couldn't go back and withdraw money from your account if you'd been there the day before. Banks simply didn't understand the day-to-day financial situations of ordinary people. Kenyans' response was to keep their money under the mattress. Fewer than one in ten Kenyan adults had a bank account at the turn of the 21st century. Today, thanks in part to Equity Bank's innovations, two-thirds of them do.

We knew we had to address the needs of people like my mother. We wanted to give banking a human face and create the concept of the bank as a marketplace where people would feel at home. We did away with high minimum balances, created affordable products, and, most importantly, delivered them where people lived.

One innovation was to introduce what we called "mobile village banking," or banking on wheels. Long before cellphone banking came along, we created mini-bank branches that could fit in the back of a Land Rover and drove them from village to village across rural Kenya. Maybe our best-known innovation, though, is our agency banking model: Equity Bank has accredited more than 30,000 small retail outlets across the country as bank agents, able to accept deposits, dispense cash, open accounts, apply for payment cards, pay bills like those for power or water, and much more.

It took us six years to convince the Central Bank of Kenya that shopkeepers could accept cash as banking agents. But once we did, we were able to multiply our network 1,000-fold. That has really taken banking to the last mile in every village. As a result, banking now competes with sugar and salt as a product.

The agency model has assisted in our continued pursuit of demystifying banking. Our agents don't talk to customers in banking jargon—they use the language of the common man in their environment. We've assisted those 40,000 shopkeepers to professionalize: they've become owner–managers, managing a bank for a commission. That in turn has distributed wealth across the country. Our business model is high volume and low margin. Cost effectiveness and efficiency are key, and technology plays an important role.

Today, Equity Bank has moved beyond Land Rovers and enabled true mobile banking via our Equitel mobile-banking application, which we launched in 2015. Equitel uses SIM overlay technology to enable easy access by customers of every mobile provider. Equitel has become very big, very fast. Today, our branches are doing 5,000 transactions a day, our agents are doing 300,000 transactions a day, and Equitel is doing 900,000 transactions a day.

As customer preferences for channels of service continue to evolve to self-service devices, the old brick-and-mortar branches are moving to become service and advisory centers. The bank's cost model is shifting from a fixed-cost to a variable-cost model. This has helped us reduce our cost-to-income ratio to an average of 49 to 50 percent, down from a high of 60 to 70 percent some years previously.

We are already looking ahead at future innovations. We see social media as the next channel for banking, so our next big focus is channel innovation. We are also looking beyond financial services and building a new business in the healthcare space—a network of medical centers called Equity Afia. The inspiration came from our charitable foundation, which has awarded some 6,000 university scholarships through paid internships to academically gifted students from across Kenya's 47 counties, under the Equity Leaders Program.

We looked at our graduates and found that 600 of them had been to medical school. We already knew that 40 percent of the defaults on our bank loans were due to ill health in the family, so we empowered our medical graduates as entrepreneur doctors, helping them start clinics and supporting them with systems to manage their clinics. At the same time, we are providing our banking customers with medical insurance.

These products intertwine the commercial interests of the bank and a solution to address the health challenge of our society. Social impact is embedded in our DNA, and it is what has enabled Equity Bank to scale: today it is the biggest bank, by market capitalization, in East and Central Africa. We see the bank not just as a company but as a movement for socioeconomic transformation. People see themselves as part of that movement. They say, "I joined, I became a member," not "I opened an account." That concept of belonging has been central to Equity Bank's growth.

Without a doubt, James Mwangi saw opportunity where many others had seen challenges. He embraced changed and pegged his strategy to the digital transformation and changed an industry and a people's way of life.

I salute the ingenuity and leadership of this brilliant man.

Fred Swaniker: Africa Leadership Academy

Fred Swaniker is the founder of several innovative educational and leadership institutions, including the African Leadership University (ALU), whose campuses in Rwanda and Mauritius are based on a new model of higher education. ALU students manage their own education, using technology, peer-to-peer learning with classmates, and four-month work-experience internships with partner companies. That enables ALU to provide a world-class education at a fraction of the cost of traditional universities. Here is Fred's articulation of his vision, his ethos and the reasons he has mapped out a digital journey that those who have followed him continue to make a difference globally.

I spend my life today looking for and developing Africa's future talent. What I can tell you is that there's an abundant source of talent in Africa: it has the youngest population in the world, with an average age of 19.5, compared to 46 or 47 in Germany and Japan. And this talent is driven, hungry, and willing to learn—all they need is an opportunity. When we give them that opportunity, even though they may have come with less preparation than you might find in other parts of the world, they catch up fast. We're able to get people who come from very disadvantaged backgrounds with very weak foundations to perform at world-class levels within two years.

Companies that succeed in Africa need to look beyond the rough edges that they might see in a young African that they interview— someone who hasn't necessarily been to a fancy university and doesn't speak English the way they might expect. They need to really invest in that talent; that investment will reap significant rewards for them as they grow.

You also have to take a strategic role in developing your own talent —to look at talent development as part of your value chain, not as something that is outsourced to the national university system. And to convert Africa's raw talent, you don't necessarily need to put people through a full four-year degree. A three-month or nine month training program could be enough to unlock the skills that companies need.

Compare Africa to India. For years, companies in India used to complain, "The universities are not producing the people we need." So companies like Infosys created their own corporate academies, and they started training and developing their own people.

Technology is a game changer in talent development. Universities, for example, were invented in a world where information was scarce, but today we live in a world where knowledge is ubiquitous. Today's technology enables an African sitting in Kenya to get access to world-class curricula and attend classes virtually from Harvard Business School, from Cambridge, from MIT. That's why we've been able to leapfrog and build the universities of the future in Africa, driving significant improvements in human-capital development with much less capital than would have been needed before.

Talent development is a critical part of the social mission of business in Africa. Because when you're in Africa, you're not just doing business, you're touching lives, you're creating meaning for your employees, you're transforming societies, and you're really creating history. Fred's legacy to the continent is a testament that it is leaders in business and not politics who will make have the greatest influence and impact for our future. Political leaders will be best served by collaborating and learning from brilliant minds such as these.

WOMEN LEADERS IN TECH

In Africa's burgeoning, male-dominated tech scene, women remain largely underrepresented. Yet there are incredible women who are launching and building successful, innovative tech companies that are upending industries, setting new standards and earning their place at the cool table. These women create and innovate, exploiting ideas, products and services to produce dynamic businesses. They are contributing innovative and even disruptive ideas, making meaningful change in people's lives.

CATHERINE MAHUGU

Catherine Mahugu is a globally acclaimed entrepreneur specializing in information communication technology (ICT) for development. She founded *Wazidata*, a design company focused on creating human-centered solutions and products that can change lives for social good. *Wazidata* has worked with Bill and Melinda Gates foundation, UNHCR and Safaricom.

She is also the Founder of *Soko*, an ethical fashion brand that expands access to economic opportunity for artisans in emerging economies. The jewellery has been featured in Vogue and Glamour Magazine. An in-demand speaker, Catherine's practical experiences and passionate delivery, have proven to be a winning formula for tens of thousands of conference attendees. She has been invited to speak by Harvard, the Economist and Financial Times.

She is an Ashoka, UN-ITU and World Bank fellow. Catherine was featured in Forbes Magazines as one of the top 30 global entrepreneurs and highlighted by BBC as one of the top 100 women. She has also been featured on CNN, CNBC, Marie

Claire, and other mainstream media. Catherine Mahugu is a globally acclaimed entrepreneur, ICT for Development consultant, keynote speaker, mentor, changemaker, youth empowerment champion and a strong advocate of gender equality and equity. She is a software engineer by profession and a change-maker by passion.

With a love of all things binary and a keen eye for design, Catherine has been involved in various ICT for Development projects. In these projects, she has applied design thinking for social innovation. She is a certified human-centered design expert, a skill acquired at Stanford University-Hasso Plattner – d.School (California, USA).

With her award-winning entrepreneurial experience, she founded *Wazidata*, a human-centred, design thinking company focused on creating human-centered solutions and products that can change lives for social good. *Wazidata* has worked with Bill and Melinda Gates foundation, UNHCR, FHI360, Quicksand and Safaricom.

Catherine Mahugu is also the Founder of *Soko*, an ethical fashion brand that expands access to economic opportunity for artisans in emerging economies. At *Soko*, she has effectively overseen the end to end operational execution and delivery of products to over 450 international retailers, several large brands such as Nordstrom, Fossil, QVC, TJMaxx, Edun, Esprit, Anthropologie and global ecommerce consumers. Notable press that has featured *Soko* products include Vogue and Glamour magazine. Celebrities such as Lupita Nyongo, Nicole Kidman, Oprah Winfrey and Emma Watson have been styled with *Soko's* jewellery. By driving and supporting the technology innovation at *Soko*, she has contributed to transforming the traditional global supply chain and changing the fashion industry for good.

Her international achievements have made her a global thought leader in matters pertaining to Africa, international trade, next generation leaders and the role ICT and women play in the entrepreneurship realm. Her impressive contribution has become a point of reference in international case studies and successful experiences to follow.

CLARISSE IRIBAGIZE: FOUNDER, HEHE LTD

Iribagize is the founder of HeHe Limited, a Kigali-based mobile technologies company that develops ways for businesses to reach their customers and audiences in a timely and affordable manner. Among other things, HeHe builds custom mobile applications for businesses, provides 24/7 online and offline support and cloud storage services. Iribagize founded the company in 2010 after winning a $50,000 grant from Inspire Africa, a Rwandan TV entrepreneurial contest. HeHe's clientele now includes African mobile telecoms giant MTN, the Praekelt Foundation and government agencies in Rwanda.

ANNETTE MULLER: FOUNDER, DOTNXT

Muller is the founder of Cape Town-based DotNxt, a company that creates, develops and delivers software, mobile, social and other digital development projects for South African companies looking for more innovative and customer-centric ways to engage with their clientele. DotNxt, which was founded in 2011, has more than 20 corporate clients including some of South Africa's largest companies such as Nedbank, Primedia and Graham Beck.

NKEMDILIM UWAJE BEGHO: FUTURE SOFTWARE RESOURCES

Begho founded Future Software Resources Ltd, a website design & web-solution provider located in Lagos, Nigeria in 2008. The company also provides online marketing, Search Engine Optimization (SEO), content management system development, online recruitment and IT consultancy services to more than 25 small and large Nigerian businesses and government agencies.

11

CONCLUDING THOUGHTS

IN RECENT years, Africa has witnessed phenomenal digital progress. Between 2010 and 2017, internet access more than doubled.

From Lagos to Kigali, from Cape Town to Nairobi, tech entrepreneurs invent medical tablets, run smartphone factories, reimagine digital finance, and empower the next generation of digital changemakers.

Investment too is on the rise. African Tech startups raised $2.02 billion in 2019, a 74% increase from the previous year.

A wind of digital change is blowing across the continent. Soon, humanity's birthplace could become a global leader in emerging fields like artificial intelligence, virtual reality, and big data. For this change to come to fruition, it will be critical to improve internet access, make capital available for tech startups, and promote good governance.

Africa's place in the digital space is unique in that most of the developments and advances are geared towards moving her forward. The pioneers of this advancement are our young people and that is one of our greatest assets. When the youth of a nation are engaged in its development, nothing can stand in its path. For years we heard that the future belongs to our youth. It seems the future is here, and our youth are ready.

We already have industry leaders among them. Leading in digital times is not difficult, Like all leadership, it calls for discipline, vision and loyalty to a cause. It is no longer business as usual and any leaders trying to lead with the old mindset will find themselves becoming obsolete.

Now more than ever, political leadership must work hand in hand with leaders in business so that together we can move forward and do so in a manner that is sustainable and all inclusive.

Like all revolutions, you cannot stop a movement and the digital migration is not an exception. Again, the term migration here is used to depict our move from doing things physically to the digital terrain. As we have seen in the book, many things have changed in the last couple of decades. Broadband exploded. Storage costs plummeted. Freemium took off as a business model. A massive wave of innovation occurred. Other tech events and trends made the many things possible. Factor in a drop in job security and a desire for people to do their own thing and suddenly it's hip to start your own company.

If we get our leadership right, both politically and in the business arena, Africa will certainly arise and the world, too, will be a better place.

ABOUT THE AUTHOR

DR. RICHIE ACHUKWU is an Author, Top Executive & Leadership Coach, Leadership Trainer, Group Coach and a leading Transformational Speaker. He is the founder of Spirit Filled Dream Coach, where he trains and empowers top coaches.

www.drrichie.solutions

He holds a Doctorate in Leadership & Management from Logos University (USA), a Certificate in Leadership Coaching from Harvard University (USA), a Certificate in Master Coach Training from the International Authority for Professional Coaching & Mentoring (UK) and a BA in Philosophy.

Dr. Richie has corporate business experience having previously worked for companies such as TRANEX Courier, DHL International as well as having consulted on Conflict Resolution & Deconfliction for Shell Petroleum in Nigeria for Chinese National Petroleum.

Dr. Richie has undertaken leadership training interventions for both the Private and Public sectors in South Africa, London, USA, Liberia, Zambia, Zimbabwe, Chad, Suriname and Nigeria etc. In South America Suriname, he has coached and trained, the Ministry of Foreign Affairs, Ministry of Communication & Transport, Ministry of Defense, Ministry of Trade & Industry and the Ministry of Regional Development.

He has also done training and coaching for the Ministry of Petroleum in the Republic of Chad, the Small Enterprise Development Agency, in the Department of Small Business, South Africa, the Gauteng Province Department of Infrastructure & Development in South Africa as well as the Richards Bay Minerals (RBM, a subsidiary of Rio Tinto South Africa), The infrastructure development department Gauteng province, among others.

He is a change agent and a transformational catalyst who uses media as a tool to reach a wide range of audiences with life transforming messages. He has hosted a live coaching feature called "The Mind Clinic" on CNBC Africa's Kicking Doors TV programme. From time to time he is invited to conduct 'live coaching sessions' on South Africa's leading TV Channel, SABC 1's Mzansi Insider programme. He also features on TBN Africa every Saturday and many more.